A COMPANION GUIDE TO

EMBRACING

GRACE

A Gospel for All of Us

SCOT MCKNIGHT

PARACLETE PRESS
Brewster, Massachusetts

A Companion Guide to Embracing Grace
2006 First Printing

Copyright 2006 by Scot McKnight

ISBN 1-55725-483-4

Scripture quotations are taken from the *New Revised Standard Version Bible*, copyright 1989, Division of Christian Education of the National Council of the Churches of Christ in the United States of America. Used by permission. All rights reserved.

10 9 8 7 6 5 4 3 2 1

All rights reserved. No portion of this book may be reproduced, stored in an electronic retrieval system, or transmitted in any form or by any means, electronic, mechanical, photocopy, recording, or any other, except for brief quotations in printed reviews, without the prior permission of the publisher.

Published by Paraclete Press
Brewster, Massachusetts
www.paracletepress.com
Printed in the United States of America

INTRODUCTION TO THIS GUIDE

The gospel is the work of our loving God to restore us in the context of a community to union with God and communion with others for the good of others and the world. Our loving God seeks to unleash the cycle of grace by embracing us so that we will learn to embrace ourselves, God, others, and the entire created order. Nothing less than this is the design of the gospel. I call this the gospel of "embracing grace" because it is the "embrace" that opens our lives to the grace that is then unleashed into our world. It is God's gracious embrace that unleashes the cycle of grace.

To understand this gospel we must begin at the beginning, with God's creating humans "in his image and likeness." An important term in *Embracing Grace* is *Eikon,* which is my expression for the "image of God." Each of us is an Eikon, and Eikons are designed to bring glory to their Maker. To bring this glory humans are given freedom to nurture their relationship with God and others, and when they genuinely love God and others, the Eikon glows. The problem, as any reader of the Bible knows, is that Adam and Eve "fell" (The story of the Fall is found in the third chapter of Genesis). That is, the Eikon cracked when humans chose (and when humans still choose) to sever their relationship with God and others. When humans do this, they are given the freedom either to embrace God and others or to exclude God and others.

The gospel of embracing grace is designed by God to lead us from being cracked Eikons to being restored Eikons who love God and others for the good of the world. But this basic definition needs one more important clarification. Adam, the Bible says, was alone, and God said that it is not good to be alone. This is why there is such a profound emphasis in the Bible on the *community of faith*. Since it is not good to be alone, and since being an Eikon means being in relationships, Individualism—the "sin of our Age"—is a path that prevents our becoming what God wants us to be. That path of restoration must be walked with others, in the context of a community of faith. The very heart of the gospel is designed to form that community. It is in that community that Eikons can be restored both to God and to others, and when that happens, we will be missionally shaped Christians who work with God for the redemption of the entire created order. The prayer for this *Companion Guide* is that it will awaken in each of us an embrace of the holistic gospel in such a way that we will become a "blessing" to the entire world.

FIVE GOSPELS OR ONE?

Before we turn to how the *Companion Guide* is organized, it might be good for us to look more closely at how the gospel is understood in the Christian world. In essence, it all comes down to "five days": the Day of Creation, the Day Adam and

Eve fell, Good Friday, Easter Day, and the Day of Pentecost. The gospel of the kingdom lets each of these days play its proper role, but many times in the history of the Church Christians have emphasized one day so much that things got imbalanced.

The Day of Creation, regardless of one's understanding of how God created, tells us that each one of us human beings is special because we are Eikons of God. Any gospel that does not begin here cannot tell the Christian story of the gospel. But, sometimes Christians have overemphasized the Day of Creation so much that the gospel is converted into a super-humanism, with humans being not only the best part of creation but the center of creation. Being special is important; being the epicenter of the universe distorts our importance.

The Day Adam and Eve fell is also important for the Christian gospel. For without the Fall there is no explanation of why humans are so amazingly inconsistent—with our wonderful mixture of glory and sin, of both goodness and badness. Furthermore, without the Fall there is no need for Christ to restore Eikons. Again, some have overemphasized the Fall and turned humans into miserable wretches, ugly on all sides, capable of no good, and doomed by God to an eternal hell. I'm not surprised by humans doing awful things, but I am surprised when I hear others suggest that humans are entirely bad. One look around will show us the good humans have accomplished—hospitals, social services, neighborly help, parental love, husbands and wives who can't wait until the other returns home, children who adore their parents.

These are witnesses to the goodness of humans, and any gospel that does not take both goodness and badness into account cannot tell the story of the Eikon.

Good Friday deserves to be at the center of the gospel. On this day, so Christians have always taught, God met humans in their utter despair and sinfulness and took all despair and sinfulness upon himself and carried it away. This is the day when Christians found guilt removed, sin cancelled, and burdens lifted. This is the day when they found that God is with them in their pain, in their suffering, and in their death. But, again, some overdo it—yes, even overdo the Cross. How? By suggesting the gospel is only about removing guilt or canceling sin or identifying with our pain. The gospel is not a tragedy, but a tragedy that turned into a comedy.

Easter is for many Christians the greatest day of the church calendar. On this day Christians celebrate not only the victory of Christ over death, but also their own promised life beyond the grave. Christians remember that on this day Jesus Christ was raised for our justification—he was raised to sit at the right hand of God to make intercession for us and to pave the way for us. Even more, on this day Christians celebrate the victory of God over systemic evil and rejoice that liberation is offered to God's people. Once again, some overdo Easter. Some forget that it is the Fall that created the need for the Death and Resurrection of Jesus, and some think so narrowly about liberation that they forget what they are liberated from: sin and self and systemic evil.

The most neglected day of all in gospel presentations is the Day of Pentecost. But it was central to early Christian thinking.

This is the day when God sent his Spirit to empower Christians to live beyond their means and to enable Christians to live in community. The early chapters of the Book of Acts are stories about what it is like for a Christian community to influence the world. But, once again, any talk about the Spirit can lead some to focus too narrowly on spiritual experiences—as if ecstasy or tongues-speaking or miracles are the point of the gospel.

No, the gospel is about the work of God to restore Eikons completely—heart, soul, mind, and strength—for the good of others and the community, so that humans will be "reunioned" with God and "recommunioned" with others. Pentecost is needed for this, but so are the Day of Creation, the Day Adam and Eve fell, Good Friday, and Easter Day. What *Embracing Grace* offers to you is a gospel that tries to keep each of these days intact and interacting with one another so much that each is present at all times.

To that end, this *Companion Guide* is designed to help each person explore all five days of the gospel.

THE IDEAL POSTURE

To benefit from the *Companion Guide* it is best if each person has a Bible, an *Embracing Grace* book, a *Companion Guide,* and a pen and paper. It is wise to spend a few minutes "centering down" (as the Quakers say) to find inner quiet to be ready both to speak with God and to hear from God. Since the *Companion Guide* is designed for a group to reflect together on the reading and on other biblical passages, it is important to be receptive to whatever the Spirit might say.

THE QUESTION OF TIME

How long might it take to do a lesson? This question is often asked of those who lead retreats and who write about spiritual formation. The answer is predictable: time is not the issue. The *Companion Guide* is constructed to help people hear from God and to help them consider changes. Sometimes we will hear from God quickly; at other times we will not. Sometimes our world will be shaken; at other times it will not be. Sometimes we will brush against Eternity in a solemn, barely detectable moment. At other times, we may struggle for days, weeks, or even months. This is how spiritual formation occurs. There are no magical formulas for union with God or for communion with others. Take all the time you need. Often you may find that the group session will not be enough; you will want to spend some time alone, in the privacy of your home, pondering items that have entered into your heart.

The wise know that what we read and what enters our mind and heart, over time, forms us spiritually. So, be less concerned with the time it takes or with obtaining immediate results than with enduring shifts in the mind and heart. Our concern is to fill ourselves with the wholesome splendor of God's Word, for it is in contact with God that our lives are spiritually formed.

Having said that, I believe that each session in the *Companion Guide* can be completed in a group session together, though some may find themselves so enrapt in prayer or meditation on a scriptural text that time will both stand still and pass in a flash. Because of time constraints some may find they will only do part of each exercise. That is fine; we are in no hurry. We are trying to hear from God. For that we have plenty of time.

BASIC FORMAT

The *Companion Guide* has a basic format: each session begins with reciting the *Jesus Creed* and ends with reciting the Lord's Prayer. The *Jesus Creed*, which I explained in my previous book, *The Jesus Creed: Loving God, Loving Others,* is this:

> Hear O Israel! The Lord is one. Love the Lord your God with all your heart, with all your soul, with all your mind, and with all your strength. The second is this: Love your neighbor as yourself. There is no commandment greater than these.

As I explained in that book, the *Jesus Creed* is how Jesus defines a spiritually formed person. A spiritually formed person, in short, is a person who loves God and loves others (for the good of others and the world) with every globule of his or her being. Because Jesus began and ended each day by reciting this text (again, see *The Jesus Creed,* ch. 1), it is an important discipline for us to follow each day, whether we recite it alone or with others. The Lord's Prayer, also explained in *The Jesus Creed* (ch. 2), is a similarly recited prayer of Jesus and his first followers. I maintain the practice of reciting both of these several times each day, and ask that those who work their way through this *Companion Guide* consider such a discipline as a form of reminding you again and again what was most important to Jesus.

Each session then works through the following: formation principle, formation prayer, formation exercises, and (for those who want to extend the session) further exploration. The *formation principle* is a summary of the theme of a single chapter in *Embracing Grace*. Someone in the group may want to summarize the chapter in more detail, while someone else may want to do the same for the biblical passages cited in each chapter. Some groups may wish to begin each session by reading one or more of the passages mentioned in the chapter.

The *formation prayer* can be prayed aloud, can be prayed silently, or can be adjusted to meet the needs of the group. The *formation prayer* is designed to turn each chapter of *Embracing Grace* into a brief prayer.

The *formation exercises* are a step-by-step process of internalizing the *formation principle* and the *formation prayer*. Genuine progress can be made by the genuinely honest. Truth telling is a non-negotiable factor for all spiritual growth because we are dealing here with our deepest selves. Another factor is just as important: for genuine spiritual formation to occur, each of us needs to be ready to change.

In each *formation exercise* we recommend that groups "identify together" specific personal connections to the *formation principle,* "reflect together" on specific items suggested from the chapter, "listen" individually to what the Lord might be saying, and "imagine" as specifically as possible how to integrate what is being learned. "Imagining" is important, because we are to love God with our minds. To do this, we must let our minds ruminate, meditate, contemplate, and cogitate (to use the classic words). And we are to let our minds wander into the wilds of God's grace. To do this, we must "imagine." We may be surprised at how much of faith begins with imagination—with vision and with wonder. Spiritual directors ask students to grow by changing, so the *Companion Guide* will ask each of us in the final group exercise to "commit" to new behaviors as an experiment of faith.

The *further explorations* section is designed for a group (if there is time) but especially for the individual who wants to follow up the group session with deeper study. I have no expectations that each person will ponder each passage each day. The various passages are given as suggested readings. Many find that "journaling" both intensifies and solidifies the session. To "journal" one needs simply to write out, either in the space provided in this *Companion Guide,* or in a notebook dedicated exclusively to spiritual journaling, what comes to the mind during the session.

Reading a chapter is rarely enough for any of us. This *Companion Guide* has one central aim: to help each of us deepen *Embracing Grace* into the soul of our being, to rub it into the tissues of our heart, and so to let it shape our entire life. Both *Embracing Grace* and this *Companion Guide* urge each of us to learn to recite the *Jesus Creed* as a daily rhythm that reminds us of the direction that God's gospel work is designed to accomplish. I know from experience that reciting the *Jesus Creed* can remind us of the center of our true vocation in life: to pursue union with God and communion with others for the good of others and the world.

PROLOGUE AND INTRODUCTION

> "The only two things that can satisfy the soul
> are a person and a story;
> and even a story must be about a person."
> —G. K. Chesterton, *On Lying in Bed and Other Essays,* 457.

Recite the *Jesus Creed* together.
Hear O Israel! The Lord is one. Love the Lord your God with all your heart, with all your soul, with all your mind, and with all your strength. The second is this: Love your neighbor as yourself. There is no commandment greater than these.

FORMATION PRINCIPLE
The gospel of Jesus Christ is for *all of us* because God loves each and every person in the world.

FORMATION PRAYER
Our gracious and loving Father, we begin our study with the hope of both learning anew and embracing anew your embracing grace. Through Jesus Christ. Amen.

FORMATION EXERCISES

• IDENTIFY TOGETHER how you and your community of faith define the gospel itself. It may be helpful to collect official church statements or tracts. What is the goal of the gospel in these official statements?

• REFLECT TOGETHER on how various Christian groups define the gospel. What is the value of understanding the gospel the way each group mentioned in the introduction to *Embracing Grace* defines it? Discuss how each definition shapes what the Christian life will focus on. Discuss how the gospel is for *all* of us. Discuss the word "embrace" as a guiding metaphor for understanding the gospel itself.

• LISTEN TO what the Spirit may be saying to you about embracing grace as a gospel for all of us. *Hear* as if for the first time what Jesus means when he says that our vocation is to love God with all our heart, all our soul, all our mind, and all our strength, and to love our neighbor as ourselves.

• IMAGINE a community in which all the churches could sit together to discuss the meaning of the gospel. *Imagine* what that could mean for the society in which you live.

• COMMIT your life to the *Jesus Creed* and to the gospel of embracing grace as your central vocation in life.

Recite the Lord's Prayer together.

FURTHER EXPLORATIONS

PONDER the following verses. You may want to *journal* your reflections in the space provided below, or in a journaling notebook.

- Genesis 12:1–3

_____
_____
_____
_____
_____
_____

- Joshua 2

_____
_____
_____
_____
_____
_____
_____
_____
_____

- 2 Kings 5

_____
_____
_____
_____
_____

- Jonah

- Luke 1:46–55

- Luke 4:16–30

- Matthew 5:3–12

_____

- Matthew 11:2–6

_____

- Acts 2:42–47

_____

- Acts 4:32–35

- 1 Corinthians 12–13

1
PERFORMING THE GOSPEL

"How can we help?"
—Pastor Mark Albrecht

Recite the *Jesus Creed* together.
Hear O Israel! The Lord is one. Love the Lord your God with all your heart, with all your soul, with all your mind, and with all your strength. The second is this: Love your neighbor as yourself. There is no commandment greater than these.

FORMATION PRINCIPLE
The gospel is proclaimed by its performance because its performance is what it really proclaims.

FORMATION PRAYER
Our gracious and loving Father, may we learn that the gospel is as much seen as it is believed, that it is as much performed as it is proclaimed, and that we are invited to reflect you and your gospel work to our local community in how we live together. Through Jesus Christ, our Lord. Amen.

FORMATION EXERCISES

- IDENTIFY TOGETHER what gospel you and your community perform by what can be seen. What are the most frequent behaviors of your community? What do those behaviors "proclaim" about the gospel? *Identify together* what your community of faith proclaims. *Identify together* your thoughts about a "come as you are culture" in a local church.

- REFLECT TOGETHER on Pastor Mark Albrecht's statement above. How does this question open up a window on what the gospel is to do in a local community and in your community of faith? *Reflect together* on the idea that the performance of a local community is its proclamation. *Reflect together* on a generation that is asking for a "come as you are" culture growing in the church itself. *Reflect together* on the stories of St. Patrick, NorthBridge, and Solomon's Porch.

- LISTEN TO what God may be saying to you about performance as proclamation. *Hear* this word of Jesus: "By their fruits you will recognize them."

- IMAGINE a community of faith that performs everything it proclaims. *Imagine* what you need to do to be part of that sort of community. No community will ever be perfect, so reflect on how it will respond as well to its imperfections.

- COMMIT yourself to performing what you proclaim. *Commit* yourself to helping your community of faith perform what it proclaims. (Without being a pest!)

Recite the Lord's Prayer together.

FURTHER EXPLORATIONS

PONDER the following verses. You may want to *journal* your reflections in the space provided below, or in a journaling notebook.

- Leviticus 11:44

- Deuteronomy 6:4–9

- Matthew 7:15–27

- Galatians 2:11–14

- 1 John 1:5–10

2
THE BEGINNING OF THE GOSPEL

*"Next to the Blessed Sacrament itself,
your neighbour is the holiest object presented to your senses."*
—C. S. Lewis, *The Weight of Glory,* 14-15.

Recite the *Jesus Creed* together.
Hear O Israel! The Lord is one. Love the Lord your God with all your heart, with all your soul, with all your mind, and with all your strength. The second is this: Love your neighbor as yourself. There is no commandment greater than these.

FORMATION PRINCIPLE
The gospel begins with this: we are Eikons of God designed by God to love God and others for the good of others and the world. When our relationships to God, others, and the world are what they can be, we "glorify God by enjoying him forever."

FORMATION PRAYER
Lord and Creator of everything, the One who created us to be Eikons, may we today learn who we are in your eyes. Through Jesus Christ. Amen.

FORMATION EXERCISES

- IDENTIFY TOGETHER the meaning of Eikon. Discuss Mister Rogers' contribution to spreading the idea of humans as Eikons; give concrete examples if possible. *Identify together* what Individualism is all about.

- REFLECT TOGETHER on the significance of freedom and relationships for being an Eikon. How does being an "accuser" or an "advocate" emerge from being an Eikon (think of the quotation from C. S. Lewis above). *Reflect together* on how Individualism prevents the Eikon from being restored.

- LISTEN TO what God is saying to you about your attitudes toward other persons who are also Eikons and to how you can learn to see others as Eikons.

- IMAGINE seeing everyone you meet as an Eikon. What difference will that make in your home, in your neighborhood, in your community, and in your community of faith? What difference will it make for how you read the newspaper or watch the news?

- COMMIT yourself to seeing yourself as an Eikon, to seeing others as Eikons, and to seeing the community of faith as designed to embrace Eikons for their restoration to God and others.

Recite the Lord's Prayer together.

FURTHER EXPLORATIONS

PONDER the following verses. You may want to *journal* your reflections in the space provided below, or in a journaling notebook.

- Genesis 1:26-27

- Genesis 2:8, 15–25

- Psalm 8

- Galatians 3:28

3
THE STORY OF THE EIKON

> Summarizing Jonathan Edwards:
> "The very essence of [God's] reality . . . was the intratrinitarian love of the Father, Son, and Holy Spirit. The only possible reason for such a perfect being to create the universe was to extend that love to other, imperfect, beings."
> —George Marsden, *Jonathan Edwards,* 191

Recite the *Jesus Creed* together.
Hear O Israel! The Lord is one. Love the Lord your God with all your heart, with all your soul, with all your mind, and with all your strength. The second is this: Love your neighbor as yourself. There is no commandment greater than these.

FORMATION PRINCIPLE
The human journey into union with God and communion with others tells the story of the Eikon: created, cracked, restored, and perfected.

FORMATION PRAYER
Our gracious Maker and Father, grant that we may see who we are by seeing who you are, that we may see who others are

by seeing who you are, and that we may live with others as your Eikons. Through Jesus Christ. Amen.

FORMATION EXERCISES

• IDENTIFY TOGETHER the reality of stories like that of Tolstoy. *Identify* the four chapters of the story of the Eikon and the importance Jesus Christ plays in understanding that story. Discuss the three dimensions of an Eikon: relationship to God, to others, and to the world.

• REFLECT TOGETHER on the relationship of the three dimensions of being an Eikon and on what the gospel is designed to do for each. *Reflect* on the significance of the *perichoresis* for understanding God's ultimate design for humans and on how we need to understand the gospel in light of the perichoresis. *Reflect* on the statement above by George Marsden about Jonathan Edwards. *Reflect* on the lines from Dante near the end of this chapter.

• LISTEN TO what the Lord is saying to you about your part in the story of the Eikon. *Hear* what the Lord says to all of us in 2 Corinthians 3:18: that we are "being transformed into the same [Eikon] from one degree of glory to another."

• IMAGINE a community of faith totally shaped by the significance of the story of the Eikon. What would the various departments of ministry look like? Imagine giving each person a "job title" in light of what they contribute to the story.

Imagine the gospel as a drawing of humans into the perichoresis of God.

• COMMIT yourself to the gospel as the story of the Eikon and to God's ultimate reality as the perichoresis.

Recite the Lord's Prayer together.

FURTHER EXPLORATIONS

PONDER the following verses. You may want to *journal* your reflections in the space provided below, or in a journaling notebook.

• Colossians 1:15

• 2 Corinthians 3:18 and 4:4

- Romans 5:12–21

- John 10:38

- Explain Mark 2:13–17 as the ministry of Jesus to restore Eikons.

4
CRACKED EIKON

"All the errors and incompetencies of the Creator
reach their climax in man."
—H. L. Mencken, *A Mencken Chrestomathy,* 5.

"Penrod and Sam were not 'bad'; they were never that.
They were something which was not their fault;
they were *historic.*"
—Booth Tarkington, *Penrod and Sam,* 107.

Recite the *Jesus Creed* together.
Hear O Israel! The Lord is one. Love the Lord your God with all your heart, with all your soul, with all your mind, and with all your strength. The second is this: Love your neighbor as yourself. There is no commandment greater than these.

FORMATION PRINCIPLE
We are not what we're supposed to be.

FORMATION PRAYER
Gracious and merciful Father, show us what we've done with the Eikon, not so we can grovel in misery or turn against the

world in ridicule, but so we can see how your grace can remake us to be what we were created to be. Through Jesus Christ. Amen.

FORMATION EXERCISES

• IDENTIFY TOGETHER what a "cracked Eikon" is and how that is important for understanding the gospel itself. *Identify* the distinction between seeing sin as "legal" or "relational."

• REFLECT TOGETHER on the comments above by H. L. Mencken and Booth Tarkington. How would you express each of those statements about humans? *Reflect* on the particular sin of a public figure and discuss how it is essentially a "relational sin." *Reflect* on Alexander Cruden as an example of Everyone.

• LISTEN TO the Lord as you would to a person and think of sins as grievances against your relationship with God; *listen to* how your sins against others are also relational. *Listen to* how your failure to care for the world is a relational sin as well.

• IMAGINE a community of faith shaped by a "sin as relationship" gospel. *Imagine* how that shaping would work itself out in gospel proclamation, in church structures, and in relations with the community. *Imagine* a community of faith that embraces "cracked Eikons" in a "come as you are" culture.

• COMMIT yourself to confessing your crackedness and to the plan of God to restore cracked Eikons.

Recite the Lord's Prayer together.

FURTHER EXPLORATIONS

PONDER the following verses and give steady attention to each as expressions of the relational nature of sin. You may want to *journal* your reflections in the space provided below, or in a journaling notebook.

- Genesis 3

- Genesis 4

- Exodus 2:11–22

Cracked Eikon

- 2 Samuel 11

- 1 Kings 8 and 11

- John 4

- Mark 14:66–72

_____
_____
_____
_____
_____
_____

_____

- Romans 3

_____
_____
_____
_____
_____

_____

- Mark 12:28–34

_____
_____
_____
_____
_____
_____

_____

5
THE EPIC OF THE EIKON

> "You two were too intent on the cat to see
> the celestial consequences of your worldly endeavors."
> —Marilynne Robinson, *Gilead,* 9

Recite the *Jesus Creed* together.
Hear O Israel! The Lord is one. Love the Lord your God with all your heart, with all your soul, with all your mind, and with all your strength. The second is this: Love your neighbor as yourself. There is no commandment greater than these.

FORMATION PRINCIPLE
Endings explain beginnings.

FORMATION PRAYER
O Lord of history, you know the End and the Beginning and everything in between; grant that we may see the End in order to know how better to live in the Now. Through Jesus Christ. Amen.

FORMATION EXERCISES

- IDENTIFY TOGETHER the various features of the End in Revelation, and any you might care to add to that list. *Identify* some Christian authors who shape the Christian life in light of how they present the End.

- REFLECT TOGETHER on how a concrete end shapes our concrete life—something from home life, something from work life, something from social life, something from a global perspective. *Reflect* together on the image of the wheel as a way of describing the End that can help us Now. *Reflect* on the statement of Marilynne Robinson, quoted above, as helping us to see how we should live in light of the End.

- LISTEN TO how the Lord wants us to see the End as shaping our life Now. How can our anticipation of union with God and communion with others as the End help us today?

- IMAGINE the End—of your relationship to God, of your relationship to others, of your relationship to the rest of creation. How much of our view of "heaven" is wish, and how much is actually found in the biblical texts?

- COMMIT yourself to an End that is defined as union with God and communion with others. *Commit* yourself to working today, playing today, and living today in light of that End.

Recite the Lord's Prayer together.

FURTHER EXPLORATIONS

PONDER the following verses as glimpses of the End. You may want to *journal* your reflections in the space provided below, or in a journaling notebook.

- Matthew 25:31–46

- Matthew 22:1–14

- Revelation 4

_____

- Revelation 21–22

6
PAGE AFTER PAGE

> See, the home of God is among mortals.
> He will dwell with them as their God;
> they will be his peoples,
> and God himself will be with them.
> —*The Revelation to St. John,* ch. 21

Recite the *Jesus Creed* together.
Hear O Israel! The Lord is one. Love the Lord your God with all your heart, with all your soul, with all your mind, and with all your strength. The second is this: Love your neighbor as yourself. There is no commandment greater than these.

FORMATION PRINCIPLE
Eikons are designed for community and therefore are restored in community.

FORMATION PRAYER
O God, the Three-in-One, you dwell in perfect interpenetrating love; you make a people to dwell in that love: draw us now into your community and into your love. Through Jesus Christ. Amen.

FORMATION EXERCISES

- IDENTIFY TOGETHER the significance of seeing God at work in community rather than at work just with individuals. *Identify* the significance of the people of God in the Bible and in the gospel itself. Consider the significance of saying the gospel is "being in the Church." Discuss the story about John Wesley found in this sixth chapter of *Embracing Grace*.

- REFLECT TOGETHER on the movements of the Bible from Creation to Revelation. What are the big events? What occupies all those pages in the Old Testament? Why is so much space given to community in both the Old and the New Testaments? *Reflect* on the statement from Revelation quoted above as the End toward which God is leading his people. Discuss the author's definition of gospel to this point. At what point in your definition of "gospel" would you insert the idea of community?

- LISTEN TO the "page after page" story of community history in the Bible, and *listen to* what this is telling us about the importance of community for the gospel.

- IMAGINE a community of faith that can say, with John Wesley, "Come and see." What would it look like? How important is the community for gospel credibility? *Imagine* a community that is credible (don't look for one that is perfect).

- COMMIT yourself to living with the community of faith as what God is doing in this world for its restoration. (Will this involve giving more of yourself to your community of faith?)

Recite the Lord's Prayer together.

FURTHER EXPLORATIONS

PONDER the following verses. You may want to *journal* your reflections in the space provided below, or in a journaling notebook.

- Joshua (or Judges)

_____
_____
_____
_____
_____
_____
_____
_____

____

- 1 Corinthians 12:1–11

_____
_____
_____
_____
_____
_____

____

- 1 Peter 2:9-10, 11-12; 5:1–11

- Acts 15

- Galatians 3:28 and 5:13–25

7
A MISSIONAL GOSPEL

> If we could think locally,
> we would take far better care of things than we do now.
> The right local questions and answers will be
> the right global ones.
> The Amish question "What will this do to our community?"
> tends toward the right answer for the world.
> —Wendell Berry, *Sex, Economy and Community*, 20.

Recite the *Jesus Creed* together.
Hear O Israel! The Lord is one. Love the Lord your God with all your heart, with all your soul, with all your mind, and with all your strength. The second is this: Love your neighbor as yourself. There is no commandment greater than these.

FORMATION PRINCIPLE
God's plan is to restore the entire created order, and he invites each of us to be co-workers in his redemption.

FORMATION PRAYER

Our Lord and Creator, you sustain the entire created order with the one word "Life!" and you invite each of us to work with you to redeem your world: forgive us for gospels that send us out of this earth, and fill us with a gospel that sends us into this earth. Through Jesus Christ, who became one of us so that we could become like him. Amen.

FORMATION EXERCISES

- IDENTIFY TOGETHER the meaning and significance of understanding "gospel" as holistic and missional. *Identify together* how beginning at the Creation narrative of Genesis 1 ties the redemption into a big gospel. *Identify* the significance of "systemic evil" for gospel work. *Identify* how you are "linking" with your world—locally and globally. *Identify* your practice when it comes to your community of faith's linking.

- REFLECT TOGETHER on how the *Jesus Creed* (Mark 12:28–32) expresses the goal of the gospel. *Reflect* on the statement quoted above from Wendell Berry and on how we are to think globally and act locally. Do you think this statement excuses us from involvement in global problems? Is there a danger here of isolationism? *Reflect together* on what you can link to in your community. Are you looking and listening enough? What can you do? *Reflect* on the dangers of turning gospel work into nothing more than social work. What makes the difference? Why do so many Christians struggle to keep gospel and social work in balance? Why do so many distinguish between the two?

- LISTEN TO the stories of what other communities of faith are doing to "link" to their communities, and *listen to* what the Lord is saying to you. What can you do? Are you listening and looking?

- IMAGINE what your community would be like if it were served properly by other local communities of faith linking to your community with the restoring power of the gospel. *Imagine* your own family linking in some way to the community. *Imagine* your family and community of faith linking to a global issue.

- COMMIT yourself today to knowing that God loves the entire created order and invites us to join him in his kingdom work of redemption.

Recite the Lord's Prayer together.

FURTHER EXPLORATIONS

PONDER the following verses. You may want to *journal* your reflections in the space provided below, or in a journaling notebook.
- Psalm 19

- Luke 4:16–30; Matthew 11:2–6

- Romans 8:18–25

- 1 Peter 2:11–3:12: notice the scope of Peter's understanding of gospel impact

---

A Missional Gospel

8
STORIES OF THE GOSPEL STORY

"Our Lord Jesus Christ, who did,
through His transcendent love,
become what we are,
that He might bring us to be even what He is Himself."
—Irenaeus, *Against Heresies,* 5 (preface)

Recite the *Jesus Creed* together.
Hear O Israel! The Lord is one. Love the Lord your God with all your heart, with all your soul, with all your mind, and with all your strength. The second is this: Love your neighbor as yourself. There is no commandment greater than these.

FORMATION PRINCIPLE
The work of God to restore us is so wide in scope and so deep in its impact that no single image can capture completely either what God does for us or what we experience of God's grace.

FORMATION PRAYER
God of wonder and grace, through your Son and the Spirit you have done all and more we could ever ask to restore us to

union with you and your world: grant us the humility to see the grandeur of your many-sided work and the grace to embrace it with our entire selves. Through Jesus Christ. Amen.

FORMATION EXERCISES

- IDENTIFY TOGETHER the meaning of each "story" of atonement. *Identify* which one best speaks your story and which one is most prevalent in your faith community. *Identify* the comprehensiveness of Irenaeus's understanding.

- REFLECT TOGETHER on whether or not you think Abelard's "story of example" is a theory of atonement. Why or why not? *Reflect* on why it is important to see "theories of atonement" as expressions of a personal embrace of God's gospel work in the person of Jesus Christ. *Reflect* on the danger of imposing one story as the dominant or exclusive story of the gospel.

- LISTEN TO the various stories of folk in your faith community and try to line up a "story" of the Atonement that most completely fits those stories. *Listen* to which story best tells your own story.

- IMAGINE a gospel presentation of each of the stories of the gospel so that each could be used to evoke how the entire Church understands the Atonement.

- COMMIT yourself to telling your own story to someone this week. *Commit* yourself to listening to the stories of other Christians. *Commit* yourself to reading the biography of one

Christian who comes from a different corner of the globe or a different church from yours.

Recite the Lord's Prayer together.

FURTHER EXPLORATIONS

PONDER the following verses and find the "story" of the Atonement that they tell. You may want to *journal* your reflections in the space provided below, or in a journaling notebook.

- Luke 4:16–30

_____
_____
_____
_____
_____
_____
_____

- Matthew 12:28

_____
_____
_____
_____
_____
_____
_____

- Luke 5:1–11

_____
_____

- John 9

- Romans 3:21–26

- Romans 5:1–11, 12–21

- 1 Peter 1:13–25

- Hebrews 4:14–5:10

- James 2:1–13

- 1 John 1

9
THE DIVINE COMEDY GOSPEL

A person dead to God cannot come to life again merely because someone else has died in his or her place."
—Francis Xavier Durrwell, *Christ our Passover,* 56.

Recite the *Jesus Creed* together.
Hear O Israel! The Lord is one. Love the Lord your God with all your heart, with all your soul, with all your mind, and with all your strength. The second is this: Love your neighbor as yourself. There is no commandment greater than these.

FORMATION PRINCIPLE
God's gospel work on our behalf involves a weekend of grace—Good Friday and Easter Morning—as well as the gift of the Holy Spirit some fifty days after the Resurrection.

FORMATION PRAYER
Lord of life, you are Life itself, and you long to share that life with us: open our hearts to receive this gift of eternal life that transforms life as we know it into a foretaste of Eternity. Through Jesus Christ. Amen.

FORMATION EXERCISES

- IDENTIFY TOGETHER the tendency to reduce the gospel work of God to the single event of the Cross. Is this true of you and your faith community? *Identify* what role the Resurrection plays in your understanding of the gospel. Discuss the statement by Durrwell quoted above. *Identify* the strengths and shortcomings of calling the gospel God's divine comedy. *Identify* some movies that are either comedies or tragedies.

- REFLECT TOGETHER on what role the death of Jesus must play in our understanding the gospel itself. Then *reflect* on what role the Resurrection must play in our understanding the gospel itself. What does each do for us? *Reflect* on how these two events must be considered inseparable in order for us to understand what the gospel is designed to accomplish. *Reflect* on their "incompleteness" until Pentecost. *Reflect* on why it is that Christians call their message "good news." *Reflect* on how the gospel of Good Friday and Easter works against systemic evil.

- LISTEN TO the gospel as Paul preached it in Romans 4: "Jesus Christ, who was handed over to death for our trespasses and was raised for our justification." *Listen* to a gospel that ends on Good Friday. Is that a "tragic" gospel or a "comedic" gospel? *Listen* to whether or not you are a "tragic" or "comedic" gospel person. *Listen* to the story of Paul Carlson in the chapter in *Embracing Grace:* what do you take away from that story?

- IMAGINE a Christian life based solely on the suffering and death of Jesus. Now *imagine* that same Christian life with the

Resurrection overcoming Jesus' suffering and death. *Imagine* a gospel presentation that speaks both of Jesus' death and resurrection: what would it look like? How does this gospel empower us to link to our communities? *Imagine* the power of resurrection for someone who needs it.

- COMMIT yourself to a gospel that descends with Jesus into the depths of sin and suffering and then ascends from that pit with Jesus into a glorious new life. *Commit* your own life to working out a fuller gospel this day—this week—in your family and your work and your community.

Recite the Lord's Prayer together.

FURTHER EXPLORATIONS

- PONDER the following verses. You may want to *journal* your reflections in the space provided below, or in a journaling notebook.
- Romans 4:25

- 1 Corinthians 15:12–19

- Peter: compare Peter's life in Mark 14: 66–72; John 21:15–23; Acts 2. How did he move from a "tragic" gospel to a "comedic" gospel?

10
A FIVE-FOOT GOSPEL

"The first man that comes into my house,
I will split his head open."
—Harriet Tubman's mother when a master
entered her house to take away her son.
—from C. Clinton, *Harriet Tubman,* 13

"For this I toil and struggle with all the energy
that God powerfully inspires within me."
—The apostle Paul, *Colossians,* ch. 1

Recite the *Jesus Creed* together.
Hear O Israel! The Lord is one. Love the Lord your God with all your heart, with all your soul, with all your mind, and with all your strength. The second is this: Love your neighbor as yourself. There is no commandment greater than these.

FORMATION PRINCIPLE
God not only releases us from our sins and gives us new life, but also empowers us to live a new life for the good of the world—even if it means a struggle against systemic evil.

FORMATION PRAYER

Almighty and gracious Father, you desire the liberation of all so that we may be united with you and in communion with all others: send once again the Spirit that inspired Harriet Tubman to empower us to fight against injustice and live the life you would have for us. Through Jesus Christ and in the power of the Spirit. Amen.

FORMATION EXERCISES

- IDENTIFY TOGETHER what it means to embrace a holistic gospel. *Identify* the three seasons of grace in God's gospel work for us. *Identify* what each does to us and for us and within us. *Identify* why it is that the Bible describes God's gospel work as "grace." *Identify* the direction of God's Spirit: what does the Spirit want to accomplish in us and through us? *Identify* the missional focus of the Spirit (see *further explorations*, below).

- REFLECT TOGETHER on the two statements above, the one about Harriet Tubman's mother and the one from the apostle Paul. *Reflect* on why it is that we need God's gracious power to accomplish what he calls us to do. *Reflect* on why Individualism is the biggest obstacle to gospel power. Discuss what Individualism would have meant for Harriet Tubman's own life.

- LISTEN TO your world's groanings for justice, *listen to* its struggles with systemic evil, and *listen to* the voice of Jesus calling us to join him in working for the kingdom of God. *Listen* to your own neighborhood's groanings—is there some place for you to link to others? *Listen to* the leading of God's Spirit to empower you to do what you might otherwise be afraid to do.

• IMAGINE a community of faith inspired by God's Spirit. What would it look like? What would it do? What would it hear, see, learn, and link up with?

• COMMIT yourself to being open to God's Spirit. Ask the Spirit of God to fill you and to guide you and to give your life the missional focus of the kingdom of God.

Recite the Lord's Prayer together.

FURTHER EXPLORATIONS

PONDER the following chapters as an exercise in what happens when the Spirit is unleashed to work out a cycle of grace. You may want to *journal* your reflections in the space provided below, or in a journaling notebook.

• Notice the missional impact of the Spirit in Acts 1–15. Trace the references to the Spirit and mark down what happens when the Spirit works. Notice how often this has to do with "reaching out" instead of just "personal holiness or love."

_____
_____
_____
_____
_____

- Galatians 3:28

- Galatians 5:13–26: notice again the Spirit's impact and its communal and missional focus.

- 1 Corinthians 12–14

11
DIMINISHED BY EXCLUSION

It was one last pathetic irony in the life of a father known mostly through absence.
—Craig Barnes, *Searching for Home,* 10.

Recite the *Jesus Creed* together.
Hear O Israel! The Lord is one. Love the Lord your God with all your heart, with all your soul, with all your mind, and with all your strength. The second is this: Love your neighbor as yourself. There is no commandment greater than these.

FORMATION PRINCIPLE
God made Eikons with the freedom to love God and others for the good of the world or to walk away from such loving relationships. The tragedy is that some exclude themselves from God and others and diminish the Eikon.

FORMATION PRAYER
Lord, be merciful to me a sinner, for I know that I exclude myself from you and from others, seeking redemption in my

own self-love instead of embracing you and others. Forgive me. Through Jesus Christ and in the hope of God's Spirit's empowering such an embrace. Amen.

FORMATION EXERCISES

- IDENTIFY TOGETHER the sheer difficulty of the human tragedy of exclusion. *Identify together* the sensitivity needed for talking about it. *Identify* ways in which you and your community of faith excludes. *Identify* any tendency to write people off as "exclusionists," when what is needed by a community that advocates grace is to overcome such a tragedy by the power of the Cross, the Resurrection, and the Holy Spirit.

- REFLECT TOGETHER on what exclusion is. Why does it diminish the Eikon? What were Eikons made for? What are some subtle forms of exclusion for you? There is a time to exclude and a time to embrace: sometimes our wounds are deep enough that we need distance to create a space for healing. Reflect on this thought. Reflect on Craig Barnes's statement quoted above; also reflect on the stories of Mary McCarthy and Tony Hendra.

- LISTEN TO the prompting of the Spirit to reveal acts of exclusion on your part. Listen to how instead of excluding yourself you might struggle to link yourself to your community and to others—and how this will awaken the memory of love.

- IMAGINE a community full of exclusionists. Imagine, with C. S. Lewis, in his *The Great Divorce,* an eternity with some seeking further and further distance from God and others. Now *imagine* a community filled with embracing people: persons who embrace God and others for the good of others and the world. Compare the first to a tragedy and the second to a comedy.

- COMMIT yourself, regardless of how difficult it might be, to a life of embracing. Commit yourself to saying the *Jesus Creed* often enough that it reminds you of when you are excluding when you should be embracing.

Recite the Lord's Prayer together.

FURTHER EXPLORATIONS

PONDER the following verses as a study of exclusion. You may want to *journal* your reflections in the space provided below, or in a journaling notebook.

- Genesis 3 describes Adam and Eve's first act of exclusion. Read the story and discuss what it tells us about exclusion.

_____
_____
_____
_____
_____
_____
_____

- Read 1 Samuel 8–16 as the life of Saul the "exclusionist." What do you see?

_____
_____
_____
_____
_____
_____

- Compare this story with David's in 1 Samuel 16–2 Samuel 24 (lots of chapters here) and notice the differences—but be honest about David's own exclusions. Read Psalm 51 as well.

_____
_____
_____
_____
_____
_____
_____

- John 6:60–71 is a good example of some who eventually exclude themselves from Jesus.

_____
_____
_____
_____
_____
_____

- Mark 4:1–20: the parable of the sower is about exclusion and embrace.

- Acts 15 is the early Christian story of fighting exclusion from within the community.

- Galatians 3:28: what kinds of prohibitions against exclusion are seen here?

Diminished by Exclusion

- James 2:1–13: what kind of exclusion do we find here?

12
ENLIVENED BY EMBRACE

We confess to you and to one another,
and to the whole communion of saints in heaven and on
earth, that we have sinned by our own fault in thought,
word, and deed; by what we have done, and by what we
have left undone.
—*The Litany of Penitence,*
The Book of Common Prayer (1979)

Recite the *Jesus Creed* together.
Hear O Israel! The Lord is one. Love the Lord your God with all your heart, with all your soul, with all your mind, and with all your strength. The second is this: Love your neighbor as yourself. There is no commandment greater than these.

FORMATION PRINCIPLE
We embrace God in return when we tell the truth about ourselves to him.

FORMATION PRAYER
O merciful, forgiving, and gracious God, you relentlessly pursue us with love: quicken our hearts, souls, minds, and strength to open ourselves to your embracing grace, that we

might be restored to you and others, and so bring glory to your gracious Name. Through Jesus Christ. Amen.

FORMATION EXERCISES

- IDENTIFY TOGETHER two or three stories of embracing. *Identify* your own story of embracing God and others. *Identify* how truth telling increases trust and even intimacy in your family and in your community. *Identify* instances in Israel's history when the people of Israel publicly confessed their sins.

- REFLECT TOGETHER on why truth telling unleashes grace. *Reflect together* on the *Litany*. Read it aloud together. *Reflect* on why (and why not in some traditions) the *Litany* is used during Lent. Discuss its appropriateness to other settings.

- LISTEN TO what the Spirit says to you as the *Litany* is read: what particular sins does it call to mind? *Listen* also to the words of forgiveness and grace at the end of the *Litany*.

- IMAGINE a community that reads the *Litany* aloud, and *imagine* what reading the *Litany* aloud can do for that community.

- COMMIT yourself to reciting the *Litany* weekly for three months. *Commit* yourself to listening carefully to its words.

Recite the Lord's Prayer together.

FURTHER EXPLORATIONS

PONDER the following verses. You may want to *journal* your reflections in the space provided below, or in a journaling notebook.

- Leviticus 16 (Day of Atonement: often called "the fast" [Acts 27:9] or "the Day")

- 2 Kings 22–23 (Josiah)

- Ezra 9

- Psalms 32, 51, and 130

- Matthew 6:7–15; 1 John 1:9; James 5:16

13
DANCING EMBRACE

*The dance of grace is first of all a dance with a person:
Jesus Christ.
—Embracing Grace*

Recite the *Jesus Creed* together.
Hear O Israel! The Lord is one. Love the Lord your God with all your heart, with all your soul, with all your mind, and with all your strength. The second is this: Love your neighbor as yourself. There is no commandment greater than these.

FORMATION PRINCIPLE

We embrace God in return when we tell God the truth about ourselves, and this truth telling manifests itself in embracing the world, the community of faith, and Jesus Christ in the sacraments through personal faith.

FORMATION PRAYER

Gracious Father, you embrace us and invite us to embrace you back: grant this day that I may embrace you and all that you are doing in this world. Through Jesus Christ. Amen.

FORMATION EXERCISES

- IDENTIFY TOGETHER the comprehensiveness of God's redemptive work. *Identify* the place of the community of faith in God's redemptive work. *Identify* your understanding of the sacraments. *Identify* the significance of *Leaf by Niggle* and show how Niggle illustrates our vocation.

- REFLECT TOGETHER on how each of the embodiments in the chapter in *Embracing Grace* needs to be an expression of a personal faith in Jesus Christ. Discuss the order presented in the book (world, community, individual) and its difference from a normal order (individual, community, world). *Reflect* on the comment from the book quoted above. *Reflect* on how complete your embrace of God's work is.

- LISTEN TO what the Spirit is saying about linking to your world, the community of faith, and the sacraments in God's redeeming work.

- IMAGINE a community of faith where each person is committed to the whole work of God in this world. *Imagine* what part you can play in the gospel work of God in this world, in your community, in your family, and in your neighborhood.

- COMMIT yourself to the world, to your faith community, and to the sacraments. *Commit* in some particular way to each.

Recite the Lord's Prayer together.

FURTHER EXPLORATIONS

PONDER the following verses. You may want to *journal* your reflections in the space provided below, or in a journaling notebook.

• 1 Peter 2:11–3:12: how does Peter see the Christian and all other relationships?

_____
_____
_____
_____

___

• 1 Peter 4:7–11: how does Peter expect the Christian to live in community?

_____
_____
_____
_____
_____
_____

___

• Romans 6:1–11; Colossians 2:9–15; Matthew 28:16–20: ponder the early Christian practice of baptism.

_____
_____
_____
_____
_____
_____

___

- 1 Corinthians 11:17–34: ponder the early Christian practice of the Lord's supper.

_____
_____
_____
_____
_____
_____
_____

14
A FAMILY OF EMBRACING GRACE

> Thus the gospel is not only good and new but,
> if you take it seriously, a holy terror.
> Jesus never claimed that the process of being changed
> from a slob into a human being
> was going to be a Sunday school picnic.
> On the contrary.
> Childbirth may occasionally be painless,
> but rebirth, never.
> —Frederick Buechner, *Beyond Words,* 137.

Recite the *Jesus Creed* together.
Hear O Israel! The Lord is one. Love the Lord your God with all your heart, with all your soul, with all your mind, and with all your strength. The second is this: Love your neighbor as yourself. There is no commandment greater than these.

FORMATION PRINCIPLE
The gospel is the power of God to restore humans, but it takes a lifetime to restore a human to being a person who loves God and others for the good of others and the world.

FORMATION PRAYER

God of patience and grace, you set out the course of history for humans as a challenge to be who you made them to be: be gracious with me as I journey this path toward union with you and communion with others. Through Jesus Christ, the perfect Eikon. Amen.

FORMATION EXERCISES

- IDENTIFY TOGETHER a story or two of strugglers who are finding their way in the path of Jesus. *Identify* whether or not you are sympathetic with strugglers. Why is it important to recognize that some people struggle with loving God and others?

- REFLECT TOGETHER on the life of the apostle John. *Reflect together* on the vision of Jesus for the kingdom of God and on what you see and don't see in yourself and in the community of faith. How does this vision relate to your society? *Reflect* on whether or not you think the story of strugglers will inhibit or encourage growth in Christian holiness and love.

- LISTEN TO the honesty of the story of strugglers. *Listen* and see if you recognize your own story in their story. *Listen to* how you can help and how you can live more lovingly in light of those stories. *Listen* and see if you are too judgmental about the stories of others.

- IMAGINE a community of faith where such stories are told without judgment but with loving concern to help others in the cycle of transforming grace.

- COMMIT yourself to accepting the grace of God as a gift that can transform you. *Commit* yourself to helping others see the grace of God as a gift. *Commit* yourself to listening to the stories of strugglers.

Recite the Lord's Prayer together.

FURTHER EXPLORATIONS

PONDER the following verses that indicate to one degree or another that the leaders of the early Christian churches were anything but perfect. You may want to *journal* your reflections in the space provided below, or in a journaling notebook.

- Acts 5:1–11; 6:1–6; 10; 15

- 1 Corinthians 1–8

- Galatians 2:11–14

- Hebrews 12

- James 3

- Revelation 2–3

- Finish with 1 John 1:9

*The grace of the Lord Jesus Christ,
the love of God,
and the communion of the Holy Spirit
be with all of you.*

—The apostle Paul
(2 Corinthians 13:14)

SOURCES/BOOKS FOR FURTHER READING

Augustine. *The Confessions.* trans. P. Burton; New York: A. A. Knopf, 2001.

Auxentios: *Eastern Orthodoxy through Western Eyes.* Louisville: Westminster John Knox, 2002.

Barnes, C. *Searching for Home: Spirituality for Restless Souls.* Grand Rapids: Brazos, 2003.

Bell, Rob. *Velvet Elvis: Repainting the Christian Faith.* Grand Rapids: Zondervan, 2005.

Berry, W. *Sex, Economy, Freedom, and Community.* New York: Pantheon, 1993.

Buechner, F. *Beyond Words.* San Francisco: HarperSanFrancisco, 2004.

——— *The Sacred Journey, Now and Then, Telling Secrets,* and *The Eyes of the Heart.* San Francisco: HarperSanFrancisco, 1982, 1983, 1991, 1999.

Burke, J. *No Perfect People Allowed: Creating a Come as You Are Culture in the Church.* Grand Rapids: Zondervan, 2005.

Carlson, P. See Lois Carlson Bridges; *Monganga Paul: The Congo Ministry and Martyrdom of Paul Carlson, M.D.* 2d ed.; Chicago: Covenant Publications, 2004.

Chesterton, G. K. *On Lying in Bed, and Other Essays.* Calgary: Bayeux Arts, 2000.

Cruden, Alexander. See Julia Keay; *Alexander the Corrector: The Tormented Genius Who Unwrote the Bible.* New York: HarperCollins, 2004.

Delbanco, A. *The Real American Dream: A Meditation on Hope.* Cambridge, Mass: Harvard University Press, 1999.

DeYoung, C., with M. O. Emerson, G. Yancey, K. Chai Kim. *United by Faith: The Multiracial Congregation as an Answer to the Problem of Race.* New York: Oxford University Press, 2003.

Doyle, B. *The Wet Engine.* Brewster, Mass: Paraclete Press, 2005.

Durrwell, F. X. *Christ Our Passover: The Indispensable Role of Resurrection in Our Salvation.* trans. J. F. Craghan; Liguori, Mo.: Liguori, 2004.

Elie, P. *The Life You Save May Be Your Own: An American Pilgrimage.* New York: Farrar, Straus, and Giroux, 2003.

Etzioni, A. "Individualism—Within History," *The Hedgehog Review* 4 (2002).

Edwards, J. *Charity and Its Fruits.* Works of Jonathan Edwards, volume 8: *Ethical Writings*; ed. P. Ramsey; New Haven: Yale University Press, 1989.

Freeman, P. *St. Patrick of Ireland: A Biography.* New York: Simon & Schuster, 2004.

Hendra, T. *Father Joe: The Man Who Saved My Soul.* New York: Random 2004.

Hollingsworth, A. *The Simple Faith of Mister Rogers: Spiritual Insights from the World's Most Beloved Neighbor.* Nashville: Integrity, 2005.

Lewis, C. S. *The Weight of Glory and Other Addresses.* Grand Rapids: Eerdmans, 1973.

Marsden, G. *Jonathan Edwards: A Life.* New Haven: Yale University Press, 2003.

McCarthy, M. *Memories of a Catholic Girlhood.* New York: Harcourt, Brace, 1957. (See F. Kiernan; *Seeing Mary Plain: A Life of Mary McCarthy.* New York: W. W. Norton, 2000.)

McLaren, B. *Generous Orthodoxy.* Grand Rapids: Zondervan, 2004.

McLaren, B. *The Story We Find Ourselves In: Further Adventures of a New Kind of Christian.* San Francisco: Jossey-Bass, 2003.

Mencken, H. L. *A Mencken Chrestomathy.* New York: A. A. Knopf, 1976.

Pagitt, D. *Reimagining Spiritual Formation*. Grand Rapids: Zondervan, 2004.
Piper, J. *Desiring God*. Sisters, Or.: Multnomah, 2003.
Plantinga, C. *Not the Way It's Supposed to Be: A Breviary of Sin*. Grand Rapids: Eerdmans, 1995.
Robinson, M. *Gilead*. New York: Farrar, Straus, and Giroux, 2004.
Shirer, W. L. *Love and Hatred: The Troubled Marriage of Leo and Onya Tolstoy*. New York: Simon and Schuster, 1994.
Sider, R., with P. N. Olson, H. R. Unruh, *Churches that Make a Difference: Reaching Your Community with Good News and Good Works*. Grand Rapids: Baker Books, 2002, which is based on R. J. Sider, *Good News and Good Works: A Theology of the Whole Gospel*. Grand Rapids: Baker Books, 1993.
Speckhard, P. A. "Who Made Thee?" *Touchstone*. January/February, 2005.
Stuhlmacher, P. *Revisiting Paul's Doctrine of Justification*. Downers Grove, Ill.: IVP, 2001.
Sweet, L. *Out of the Question—Into the Mystery: Getting Lost in the God Life Relationship*. Colorado Springs: Waterbrook, 2004.
Tarkington, B. *Penrod and Sam*. Bloomington, Ind.: Indiana University Press, 2003.
Tolkien, J. R. R. *Tree and Leaf*. Boston: Houghton Mifflin, 1989.
Tolstoy, L. *A Confession*, in *The Portable Tolstoy*. ed. J. Bayley; New York: Penguin, 1978.
Tubman, H. See Catherine Clinton, *Harriet Tubman: The Road to Freedom*. New York: Little, Brown, 2004.
Vanhoozer, K. "The Atonement in Postmodernity: Guilt, Goats and Gifts," in *The Glory of the Atonement: Biblical, Historical, and Practical Perspectives*. Downers Grove, Ill.: IVP, 2004.
Volf, M. *Exclusion and Embrace: A Theological Exploration of Identity, Otherness, and Reconciliation*. Nashville, Tenn.: Abingdon, 1996.
Webber, R. *The Younger Evangelicals: Facing the Challenges of the New World*. Grand Rapids: Baker Books, 2002.

Wesley, J. *John Wesley.* ed. A. C. Outler; New York: Oxford University Press, 1980.

Yancey, Philip. *What's So Amazing about Grace?* Grand Rapids: Zondervan, 1997.

Zacharias, Karen Spears. *Hero Mama: A Daughter Remembers the Father She Lost in Vietnam—and the Mother Who Held Her Family Together.* New York: William Morrow, 2005.

ABOUT PARACLETE PRESS

WHO WE ARE

Paraclete Press is an ecumenical publisher of books on Christian spirituality for people of all denominations and backgrounds.

We publish books that represent the wide spectrum of Christian belief and practice—Catholic, Orthodox, and Protestant.

We market our books primarily through booksellers; we are what is called a "trade" publisher, which means that we like it best when readers buy our books from booksellers, our partners in successfully reaching as wide an audience as possible.

We are uniquely positioned in the marketplace without connection to a large corporation or conglomerate and with informal relationships to many branches and denominations of faith, rather than a formal relationship to any single one. We focus on publishing a diversity of thoughts and perspectives—the fruit of our diversity as a company.

WHAT WE ARE DOING

Paraclete Press is publishing books that show the diversity and depth of what it means to be Christian. We publish books that reflect the Christian experience across many cultures, time periods, and houses of worship.

We publish books about spiritual practice, history, ideas, customs, and rituals, and books that nourish the vibrant life of the church.

We have several different series of books within Paraclete Press, including the bestselling Living Library series of modernized classic texts, A Voice from the Monastery—giving voice to men and women monastics on what it means to live a spiritual life today, and Many Mansions—for exploring the riches of the world's religious traditions and discovering how other faiths inform Christian thought and practice.

Learn more about us at our Web site:
www.paracletepress.com, or call us toll-free at
1-800-451-5006.

ALSO AVAILABLE FOR SMALL GROUP STUDY

Discover how the Jesus Creed of love for God and others can transform your life.

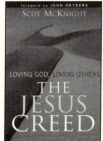

The Jesus Creed
Scot McKnight
350 pages
ISBN: 1-55725-400-1
$16.95, Trade Paper

When an expert in the law asked Jesus for the greatest commandment, Jesus responded with the *Shema,* the ancient Jewish creed that commands Israel to love God with heart, soul, mind, and strength. But the next part of Jesus' answer would change the course of history. Jesus amended the *Shema,* giving his followers a new creed for life: to love God with heart, soul, mind, and strength, but also to love others as themselves.

"An excellent introduction to Christian spirituality. Its pages glow with compassion, generosity, and the invitation to understand what was important to Jesus and what is crucial for Christianity."—*Publishers Weekly*

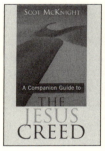

A Companion Guide to *The Jesus Creed*
Scot McKnight
80 pages
ISBN: 1-55725-412-5
$5.95, Trade Paper

Used by more than 1000 churches in 2004/2005!

According to Jesus, the spiritually formed person is the one who loves God and who loves others. This *Companion Guide* enables the reader to anchor the lessons of *The Jesus Creed* into the depths of one's heart. Each day's *Guide* applies the fundamental spiritual formation principle of each chapter in *The Jesus Creed*, and then encourages us to dig deeper in the Gospels to learn more about how *The Jesus Creed* shaped the life of Jesus and all those around him.

Available from most booksellers or through Paraclete Press
www.paracletepress.com • 1-800-451-5006.
Try your local bookstore first.